Waiting Places:

Poems of Advent Seasons 1969-2016

By
David J. Adams

Blue Shale Books

Copyright © 2016 by David J. Adams.
All rights reserved.

Published by Blue Shale Books.
Moreland Hills, Ohio

Library of Congress Control Number: 2016918139
Adams, David J., 1946-

Cover Image: "Winter Evening", by Zilla Sussman. Print, circa 1971. Property of the Author.

Author Photo: "David and Rosie", by Tom Adams. 2015

Acknowledgements:

As noted in the Introduction, some of these poems (at least versions of them) were collected in earlier volumes, including the following: *Another Place*. 1980. Stone Country Press. *North into Love*. 1984. Quarry Press. *Where We Came In*. 1992. Bottom Dog Press. *First Light*. 2001. Lost Shadow/Goose River Press. *Evidence of Love*. 2004. Finishing Line Press. *Room for Darkness, Room for Light*. 2009. Blue Shale Books. *Looking the Other Way*. 2013. Blue Shale Books.

Individual poems first appeared in the following journals or magazines: *Angel Face, Centennial Review, Kennebec, Laurel Review, Maine Sunday Telegram, North American Review, Off the Coast, Penumbra, Stone Country* and *Quarterly West*.

For my parents, Louis and Carolyn Adams, for
my mentor and friend Fred Eckman, and for all the angels,
living or passed on, who have inspired or
otherwise inhabited these poems.

Introduction

In *Waiting Places: Poems of Advent Seasons, 1969-2016*, David Adams is a contemporary Wise Man following his star over forty years and across the northeastern part of America along highways from Maine to Michigan via the Southern Tier of New York State and the northern coast of Ohio, seeking in places and in memory, hoping against all reason, to find the meaning in them.

Following his *Room for Darkness, Room for Light*, New & Selected Poems 1972-2008 and *Looking the Other Way*, New Poems 2008-2013, he has gone back to collect his meditations on the liturgical season of Advent written regularly, almost as a discipline, over more than 40 years. Taken together, they record both a quest and a series of tributes: to places, to ordinary people known and simply seen, and from memories of a Catholic upbringing through a metaphysical swerve that finds immanence in the natural world: woods, water, sky, and, always, stars.

The apparent ease with which real American places (with their serendipitous Classical and Biblical names) and subjects (animals, parents, children, lovers) morph into symbols of the human desire for an answer to all that questions is a tribute to Adams' patient, careful eye, as he observes, looks inward, then upward to the stars.

Whether on the Boston subway (Orange Line), a trail in the Cuyahoga Valley National Park, or—perhaps my favorite— The Blue Water Bridge that links Port Huron, Michigan, and Sarnia, Ontario, at the influx of the strait that empties the upper Great Lakes into the lower ones, Adams travels, looks, and ponders what he sees. The symbolism of the bridge—crossed, he assures us twice, by 2 million travellers a year—under which passes a freighter and its crew bound for Duluth, the northernmost port for the American industrial heart (the ore that makes the steel that makes the cars that cross these bridges), is powerful all the more because it is totally implicit. Alongside the poet, we discover the connections ourselves.

It seems that for Adams the weeks leading up to Christmas (and in these poems, sometimes all the way to the Feast of the Epiphany) are frequently times of travel, of driving from temporary homes to the "home" remembered from childhood, often at dusk or darkness, in those numinous moments when dreams seem real and regrets or hopes emerge to prick us. It's certainly possible to see the Advent Poems as a distillation of Adams' poetry overall, in which the themes and styles—lyric narrative or "persona" poems in a conversational style that elevates the music and imagery to a plane where archetypes emerge—are most plainly presented. The baby Jesus never arrives in these poems, only the sacredness of what Randall Jarrell called "the dailyness of life."

—Suzanne Ferguson,
Samuel B. and Virginia C. Knight
Professor of Humanities, Emerita
Case Western Reserve University

Preface

I must thank Suzanne Ferguson for her thoughtful and generous Introduction. Perhap it may help to explain what I've been doing all these years. What started a very long time ago as a seasonal gesture for friends became a habit of reflection and construction. The poems in this collection are mostly, but not exactly, chronological. Some were not "official" Advent poems, but were spinoffs or simply relatives of the official poems, written about the same time. As Suzanne notes, some poems were, like hopefulnss itself, a little late in arriving.

I think that not just in these times, but in any times, hopefulness can be difficult to sustain as the drowning cacophanies of wealth and power, and the storms of their pusuits, surround us with incessant and virulent noise. Maybe the difficulty is a matter of, to paraphrase the old country song, "Looking for hope in all the wrong places..."

Many years ago a rural pastor with a degree in divinity from Princeton explained to me the importance of the present imperfect in Biblical Greek. *Be seeking, and you shall be finding*, or words to that effect. That concept has never left me. I never wanted these Advent poems to be merely an annual exercise, some labored version of Philip Larkin's weary lines "surprising...a hunger...to be more serious." Call them a habit, a gift for those who want them, a vehicle for a way of seeing the world as best I can. Seeing them together, walking through them and their years, has been a journey both somber and joyous. Suzanne Ferguson offered that some of the poems are "difficult." I hope this habit of writing notes for some of the poems will help a bit.

Notes on the Poems

Lights, 1954 — When I was a child, driving to see the elaborate displays of lights in the yards of the "folks with money" became a family tradition. Add to those homes the wonderful decorations in General Electric's Nela Park facility, and the trip veered into a kind of fantasia of everything associated with the season.

Letter — I wrote this poem as Christmas approached me in a season of dissonance in my life. The "letter" points back in time to a shared experience of working winter night shifts in a gas station in Toledo, Ohio. Somehow, writing about that shared connection became a source of hope.

Crossing the Hudson in a Whiteout: 1994 — I lived in New England for over 25 years, which meant many holiday trips home across I-90. Several of the poems here reflect those journeys. Anyone who has made that trip in winter knows the special chill that comes from hearing the words "lake effect" in a forecast. *Schelomo* is a concerto for cello by Ernest Bloch.

Advent at the Looking Glass River — When one lives beside the Looking Glass River, as I did in Michigan, almost any dream is possible.

Winter Laundry — My friend the singer and songwriter Chris Stuart once called me a "drive-by poet." He later recanted. But in the case of this winter scene in Maine, he would have been right—with the necessary qualifier that the actual by itself is seldom sufficient for making a poem.

In Its Season — How does a poem provide hope, much less solace, to a friend who has lost a daughter in a terrible accident? In this case the beloved girl was as much a true "nature girl" as could be imagined. So the poem had to go there.

Sun and Moon with Wounded Swan — I have long had a special affinity for the sky in which the sun and moon appear together, both in real life and in large painted screens I viewed in an exhibit called *The Triumph of Japanese Style*. As with "Letter", this poem was a reaching out to offer something like hope to a friend in turmoil.

True and Untrue at Christmas — "True and Untrue" is the title of a Norse folk tale in which the two brothers have those names. That tale had fascinated me since childhood, and over the years I had many aborted efforts to use it in a poem. The moral of this version: don't invite a poet home at Christmas.

Kiska's Taste in Turds — Another I-90 poem. I'm afraid if you wonder why this poem fits in the collection, you are missing an especially precious connection with our fellow creatures that has always been, for me, at least, a continuing source of hope.

In Advent — After my father died, I couldn't write even a line for the better part of a year. Then this Advent poem appeared. Through many years he had told me that hope is something we construct, and he knew a thing or three about construction.

The Shortest Day of the Year — Written "in voice", this poem grew out of a dream I was told by someone dear, but the poem is mostly invention.

Advent at the Port of Galilee — Galilee is a fishing village at the southern tip of Rhode Island. In cold early December, when the tourists had all left, George's of Galilee is a seafood restaurant from which a window seat afforded a good view of the purse seiners riding the evening tide home. What would poets do without windows to get them started?

Advent at the Hospice of the Western Reserve — I wrote this poem in December of 2011 when my mother was brought to David Simpson House right on Lake Erie. "In the Bleak Mid-Winter" is a moving hymn set to words by Christina Rossetti.

An Advent Dream Begins in Majuro — Majuro is the island capital of the Republic of the Marshall Islands. I had been there many times, but in 2014 for the first time during Advent. As usual, when dealing with hopefulness and dreams, one thing leads to another.

Contents

Acknowledgements: i.
Introduction ii.
Preface and Notes on the Poems iv.
Christmas 1969 9.
A Dream of Christmas 10.
Covenant 11.
Letter 12.
Lights, 1954 13.
December, 1949 14.
Friday 15.
Fantasia on an Advent Theme: Hallowell, Maine 16.
Crossing the Hudson in a Whiteout: 1994 18.
A View of Advent from High Street: Hallowell, Maine 19.
Advent at the Looking Glass River 21.
Sun and Moon with Wounded Swan 22.
Under the Same Sky 23.
Winter Laundry 24.
In Its Season 25.
The Position of the Moon at Christmas 26.
A Geography of Christmas 27.
The Shortest Day of the Year 28.
To a Magic, Joyous Kingdom 30.
An Advent 32.
Driving across Southern Michigan in Late
    November: 1973 37.
A Hunter in a Tree Stand: Allegany County 38.
Advent Thoughts: Perry City Road 40.
Advent from the Blue Water Bridge 42.
In Advent 43.
Faces on the Orange Line 41.
The Music of Advent at North Station 45.
True and Untrue at Christmas 46.
The Feast of the Epiphany at North Chagrin 45.
Question for the Mind of Winter 46.

Kiska's Taste in Turds   47.
The Light of Advent Falls across Sandusky County   48.
A New Year in the Empire of Shadows   50.
Song for the Winter Solstice at Chagrin   51.
Advent at the Port of Galilee   52.
Advent at the Hospice of the Western Reserve   53.
An Argument of Hope along a Passage to the Allegheny   54.
Indications of Advent on LaDue Reservoir   56.
An Advent Dream Begins in Majuro   58.
The Effect of Snow on Dreams   59.
Advent Graves at All Souls Cemetery   60.
Advent Dreams in the Garden of Snows   62.
Advent in a Wind of Memory   64.

Christmas 1969

The snow, like moon sand,
sticks to everything,

Christmas fashion,
the yard below wrapped

like a soul in tissue.
My eyes sweep stars

uncountable until
the dawn will swallow

all their light in cloud
until it seems there is

not a place to stand.
Neither child, nor elf,

nor a shepherd
in his rags,

I am either out of season,
or there is no season.

A Dream of Christmas

On my street, at dusk, I watch
the houses switch on Christmas,
like a caravan of light that winds
beneath the northern sky.

Memory tells its children once more
a riddle that is joy, its answer
buried in the arc of years.

She sleeps, a star flowering
in her ear pressed low upon a pillow.
If she wakes and rubs the dust

of lights from her fingers, would she
have called the star eternity,
a story in a language all her own?

Before the relatives with gifts.
Before the breaths of hams in candy,
the sweet and smoky air,

before the darkness of waiting,
the child remembers.

Covenant

I stare at the frozen lake
and the snow upon it like sand;
the relentless wind recites
the cold chant of old earth.

But the dream of lions comes.
They are lying in a garden, gold,
and small as cats' paws,
with eyes of flaming oil.
I put the lions on the tree,
make my wish and go to sleep
as the tree burns.

The lions wake me gently
with their tongues, and lead
me where the star has fallen
and flares in the parched grass.

Letter

Friend,
The walnut in my yard is dying;
its stark shadow rhymes with the sun
against my door.
You can stand in the cleared lot
across the road and look. Look.
Look for a face in the window
framed by yellow bricks.
I am painted into a duplex in Virginia.
More still-lives than we can cure
with surprise alone.
I watch the leaves fashion a dry sorrow
on the walk and the dead lawn;
I have dreams. I remember
the salt that seemed to climb
from the slush to paint my uniform.
Windshields shattered from the cold;
the orange sun a brittle sign,
neon in the blue dusk.
Here my neighbor's children
chase their small shadows
across the afternoon.
An old, dark Ford breathes by them
with something like caution,
frightful as a lie.
We do what we can. What we can.
Watch, then. Is it your face or my own,
rust from the wind's cold tears?
Put something down
Stop standing there.

Lights, 1954

A family will go to see the lights.
They finish their Christmas fish,

and from the cold car's black
windows, the child searches

the stars for a star, a promise
of the wrapped, glittering dawn.

In the Heights the yards and homes
are lit like fairs. Touching the glass

with his fingers, his small cheek,
he loves what is loved.

No one could sleep, yet he dreams
he is carried to sleep,

of a radio choir. On the lawn
of his dream the lost angels

return as shepherds, and his eyes
water down the cold window.

Lights! Lights!

December, 1949

He lies upon the settle bed,
napping in his cousin's overalls,
feeling memory advance as furtively
as breaths of pressure
from the plated iron of the radiator
blown to where he wakes.
The room is blue as clay with
cakes of china high above the mantle.
However old I am, it is enough
to lead him to the French doors
of the balcony, his legs like pillows
in the bulky corduroy.

One story far below, the evening world,
its animals, a December we approach
as if it were another room. Black sedans
rake furrows in the snowy boulevard.
A streetcar's clack and bell,
a yellow plume with sparks.
In the yard a single squirrel
digs into the ice beneath a sycamore;
across the way the windows
shrink their Christmas fires
to trees and wishes.

Dark enough, a window is a mirror.
Already he has moved enough from sleep
to play with what he sees,
and calculates which eye is best
for this, his cheek rolled flat
against the frigid pane.

Friday

> *"Longing beyond beauty to the vacant sky."*
> -Frederick Eckman

Beneath my office window
and across the road sundry
women are filing to a church bazaar,
where they will become unhinged
at the tables of chocolates
like an act of weather.
A little beyond, sunlight blinks
in the green aluminum wreathing the stores.
One fat pigeon steps the cornice of the bank.
I could go on. There are mountains
out there. I wanted it to be Friday;
I remember the very wish.

Fantasia on an Advent Theme: Hallowell, Maine

Where houses rub their sallow eyes
to comprehend the long night's storm,
whose drifts are shadowed dark as plums.

Where pickups idle at the market,
the milky plumes of their exhausts.
For those awake the cold has starred
the day with circumspection—
coffees steam in paper mugs
held close as votive candles.

Where two mergansers on the Kennebec,
skirting skim ice with the grace of mists,
are too common to disperse the wait
for some more central miracle—
to know the Universe has changed.

Where, later, an arrow of the sun
will pierce the cataracts
of one hinged man who shovels hopelessly
a corner of his walk. Beyond,
a fir is leaned against the garage.
As a child in one lost dream
he brings a new cross to St. Basil's,
its three bells caroling
the fiercest cold of history.

Where up and down the streets of town
graupel lofts from spruce like incense.

Where, all along the sills of shops,
bulbs blink among the boughs.
To wish, to pray, to dream, to wait —
to walk among the weathers
where light has warmth, not mercy.

Crossing the Hudson in a Whiteout: 1994

I could touch you so easily,
it seemed, reaching back four hundred miles
through darkness, your sky still clear.
One hand on my shoulder.
One hand pointing to a star.

Around me gusts of snow occluding
girders, hissing softly on the cab.
The taillights of a semi flashing dimly,
hovering in air like angels
on the verge of anger at a world
whose blue tracks disappeared
so randomly as weather,
the forecast chants a cold reprise:
nine hours of wind and snow ahead.
You see, I was going home without you
On that northern, beaten path.

Two nights later, seated in a hall
amidst the pressed warmth of an audience,
Schelomo played as if it were an atmosphere
whose ghosts had settled in my breath,
my heart, now that it all is memory—
each year ending, and its dangers
shaken in a gourd to whisper:
When, precisely, was it you believed?

A View of Advent from High Street: Hallowell, Maine

Jogging the long hill—past renovated Capes,
arborvitae, maples stripped to black obelisks,
a barking spaniel—my breath a little furnace
as I pad along this cold, gray arm that
clutched the highest granite it could find.

Westward, buried in rolling fields,
a chainsaw rages at something
harder than the blue air.
Below, bordering a Toyland,
the black channel of the Kennebec
winds through its ice like an open vein.

These ways the world demands attention
to its sense of keeping watch.
I remember, as I run,
taking down a chest of ornaments,
a liturgical scent of wax so near…
confusing years with thinking of years.
And then Christmas as an answer.

Now who hears the saw, the breath,
the spaniel, the bass note of my heart
as parts in a worldly round, that is,
a world in which one shepherd
pulls tighter at his skins, feeling
the least freshening of wind?
Seasons! Checking for traffic,

I turn toward home.
These river lives, and the trees and I
all breathe this present imperfect world…
Be seeking…Be waiting…Waiting.

The snow comes sudden as I coast downhill.
In one yard a woman leans out from a ladder
to hang her lights and boughs above a window
and drops a hammer with a rising curse. *Oh damn!*
Inside, pressed against the dark glass,
Her little one is pointing at the sky.

Advent at the Looking Glass River

He seldom dreams of what he sees,
but the street lamp's moon is growing in his eyes
like an orchid that the world flows past.
He stares at the black mirror of the river
until the stars appear at last.

From up the hill the carols float to him
among the bursts of snow.
White dwarves, red giants—is each
An angel still, all in flight beyond their names?

Once he thought to watch would be enough;
a watcher never lacks a reason, never needs a dream,
as if the story by itself could heal—
the boy spilling wax upon the cassock
is saved as is the thief, if only…

He helped his father tie the boughs to wreaths.
Another, dreaming, says to his friend,
"Did you see the old man on the bridge?"

He seldom dreams of what he sees,
but the darkness that he wakes to is familiar.
Outside the locusts still join hands upon the snow,
and the crows that watched him home
sleep in pines without a wish.

In the dream the boy says, "Father, do we
go to heaven, or does it come to us?"
In the room his dog sighs once
and closes its black eyes.

Sun and Moon with Wounded Swan

Here your wounded voice floats hours
past the telephone, trapped like a dream
in the interstices of wind and light,
a slow accumulation we can almost see.

So listen, that tender habit something
so like love, like hopefulness,
and search the sky above
the swaying brooms of reeds
and find the sun and moon—
a blazing hand, a faded coin—
balanced in the vacant blue.

It means something, as if standing
in some larger soul's geometry,
that lone swan drifting, its torn wing
slumped an inch or two, unable
to conceal the dark brown sash of injury.

Still, tilted as a broken bob,
it dips to snatch the frozen grasses,
while in a line across its tail
two others struggle in a slow ascent,
their wingbeats like a bellows.

Will you listen with me
to the morning as it paddles near?
A blade of something dangles
from its beak, its eyes like anthracite.

Under the Same Sky

Midnight through the window
where he boils water for his tea.
The clouds assemble as dark wounds
he feels as possible dreams.
Is she dreaming, adding
the mark of a year to her sleep
under the same sky
that leans to him through the black panes?
He is so late in his chair
the dog gets up to wonder.
Steam from the cup has started something
as grey as her eyes. He is waiting
again, and he knows it.
Far, far away.

Winter Laundry

She appears on the wooden porch, her arms filled with a rubbish bag distended with wet laundry. She makes several tries at pulling shut the door with the elbow of her coat before setting down the bag and reaching to the handle. From inside blares the noise of her immunity, her little sons fighting over programs.

When she closes the door there is only the sound of wind. Her black coat widens as she bends to lift the bag, to hold it as if it were a huge, soft pumpkin. Her own thickness and the weight of wet clothes and the bitter wind make walking difficult.

She makes her way across the crusted mud of the yard to the laundry line. How little warmth the sun gives. Even the glare from the dead fields hurts her eyes.

Already the clothes are stiff, and she works more quickly than one could believe—pinning the clothes, moving sideways, dragging the bag beside her. The shirts and jeans and towels sway like colored boards. One large sheet is still soft enough to flap. She is nearly done. Wind tears the water from her eyes that, like her visible flesh, seem to have no color at all.

The empty sand truck highballs around the curve like an orange bull gone mad, veers to the shoulder and raises the dust to a cresting wave. Then, more of a cloud, the rising cumulus of dirt hesitates, bursts across her yard. She coughs twice and turns. Her smallest one is yelling through the open door.

In Its Season

It is nearly true winter, but only enough
snow to cover some of the headstones
over which the mourners troop, trying
to keep their balance on the pillowed ground,
in the shifting wind, so that we might
have tears just standing here even
without this young death we feel as
a weather from which there is no indoors.

The spray of pine and cones upon the casket
like a wreath upon a door to call us
to a season counting its birth of hope.
If she lit her hope to candles, they are
as distant now as stars, as cold
as stars seem. It is wrong.
Being human, we want a thing to blame.

So let us blame the sky. Looking back
from this graveyard, along the valley
of the Carrabassett, we see it too is wrong,
racing blue and copper as a thunderstorm
August in its danger. In its season
the storm never quite in us breaks.
We gather and disperse, crunching and
sliding to our cars, wordless in early night.

Later, when the sky has begun to clear,
when snow has drifted to the fresh earth,
in her deep, blue forest beyond her grave,
a doe has stood from its needles
and turned its ear to the wind.
Through the boughs, frozen in a dark eye,
the light of one star made near.

The Position of the Moon at Christmas

Worn coinage of a moon, ascending
the black branches of trees
frozen to the snowless grass,

my almanac predicts the angles
of your light this season,
the rippling degrees of flattery
that light obeys.

While outside,
in the stiff lawn, the uncollected
apples stick like broken coal.

Your light should be less careful;
each year you are outdistanced
in revelation.

Waiting, waiting, waiting:
salvation will be ruthless.

Tonight, as you step from the high branch
and mix your outcome with the stars,
in your measurements no one is accounted for;

but what is clear by you
is clear at last.

A Geography of Christmas

Hours past the first snow of the season
the sun has left an orange and purple braid
along the ridges of the Cuyahoga.
Is this just the usual retreat that promises
another day, or has the snow
caught fire on the hills?

Such fire, captured, is the stoplight
under which a woman leads her husband
to their Saturday confessions.
In an overcoat, galoshes, and a babushka
dark as spruce, she tugs him like a frozen hinge,
their joined hands bobbing in the fading light.
Shrunken between his scarf and cap
a face of onion skin, his spectacles askew.
His stiff gait pulled towards absolution.

Beyond them, in tableau, two men
are working at the crèche. One lays pine
amidst the Holy Family; the other turns
a spotlight to the Star of Bethlehem.

Far elsewhere at that very hour
a young man sorts the northern heavens,
hoping, and steps from snow and birches
to a frozen lake. Each black branch
he heaves above the ice spins loose
a carol's whisper to a ghostly star,
falling, that is not his star.

The Shortest Day of the Year

Here, at last, the least light of the year
reaches into my day on the bright, cold wind,
winter come too soon for me to be quite ready.
If once there were a thread between
the light and the season, a way
of knowing something...
it was so long ago.

Here the drafty snow is buzzing
in the spruce outside my window,
stinging chickadees, and below
my daughters, clothed as my sweet birds,
are running, tracing in the snow
the circles of a game I taught them once.

These years that start and end
with the northern earth leaning
from its lights have been my habits.
I love to watch them playing, already they
have claimed so many of my years as theirs
that something fearful stings my fingers
when they play in someone else's yard.

One night in a dream I watched them
circling my heart in the snow,
tumbling till they cupped it like a crystal
red on their four mittens, snow melting on it.
There was a wind like this.

As the day retreats, and they laugh
in the shrinking light,

I think of my heart in their hearts,
a swallow racing in a purple sky.
Down my street are the familiar yards,
trees that never seem to change, not even grow.
And yet, it's different, the fall of light
across two cedars broken in an August storm.

And should I fix upon a neighbor's broken shingle?
Such small distinctions trouble me
as the sudden draft from a door downstairs.
The girls are in for cookies. They have
grown up around me and now—
laughing too loud, slamming cupboards,
snow still flaking from their jeans—
they are my joys run wild, a scene
as clear as any I could dream.

Hearts like birds, like red apples. Perhaps
an old hag hangs outside the door.
Oh what a world!
Mirror, mirror, bring me the news...
What was broken in the storms of my own years,
cutting the view to emptiness,
wishes plain as frozen pools?
The years have a place for everything.

What do they see, I wonder, when they look at me?
My white face aging like a house,
that fading trace of moon out there so cold.
Oh Lord, a small bird's silver wing.

To a Magic, Joyous Kingdom

I.
Far beneath December's moon,
three trailing wisps of snow
the only evidence an owl has left its bough
to glide across the carpath's trackless way,
a faintest kiss of pine on sycamore.

The house that ends this path
is built so deep in woods
it has to be a house of tales
that only animals or elves could find.

On this night it sits as still as coal
wrapped tight in frozen laurel,
but in its darkness someone sleeps
twisted in his quilts,
his murmur like a dreaming hound's.

The book abandoned to the chance of dreams
lies open on his table.
The picture there of Stalingrad,
whose earth seems white as sand,
where flesh and rubble have attained
a rough equivalence as ornament.
In the corner where the sky would be
a flare hangs senseless as a star
that follows him to sleep in which
the owl is eating something it has killed.

To wait upon the world's illumination
he will sleep, then wake, and burn
his life the way a stove burns air.

II.
Later, the creek that tumbles from the falls
is frozen at its edges.
Standing on a mound of shale,
he sees his dog discover ice
and pinwheel like a furry mop.

A dark wire in the sky drifts near
above the lake and lightens
to a wedge of geese who mourn
their knowledge of the air.

The dog is up and yapping
at the burbling stream as if
all ice were treachery,

while the geese have sunk
into a blue rim of cloud above
the other shore, for now invisible,
the sad refrain of those who
always find the world they seek.

Driving across Southern Michigan in Late November: 1973

These fallow, matted fields stream by,
soaked and colorless as sponge.
Not even a crow to glean.
The sun behind me closing like an eye.

Hunters pass me in their pickups,
speeding home. In one,
an orange vest draped across the gun rack,
the cab fluorescent from the instruments.

It is late enough;
the lamps of houses blink like ships
adrift among the blackened groves.

Far ahead, burning rose and white,
the constellation of a water tower.
Passage here is dark and decimaled
as tires on the asphalt
hum a late, reluctant lullaby.

Nearly everywhere outside my warm machine
blood's traffic slows to dreams.
The time invented for waiting
is at hand.

An Advent

On this day so unspeakably clear the
sky is white in one direction,
dividing the planet I live from life.

A hawk might drift across an eye
aloft for years, it seems.
It is nearly Christmas again.

My neighbor's children
drag their spruce across the arctic yard
like puppies with a twig too large.

The broken needles in the snow
mark the path they will never take again
as who they are. It will be different.

When night comes, and wind
I remember, too, how it is.
The watched sky shrinks to stars.

A Hunter in a Tree Stand: Allegany County

The Southern Tier Expressway falls beneath
the ridges deepened by the paltry sun.
There a tongue of fire girds a maple
and grows into a man whose shotgun
rests across his knees, his whole repose
like a sad gourd hardened to eternity.

For he has waited hours, that is, for years
while the snow has drifted trackless
in the clearing ringed with pine because,
as he is now a memory,
he has remembered through the empty hours
what his patience yields—if not
his target, then his life.

Now, from his window, he follows
as his mother sings the steaming cows
into the barn, and the frozen mud
is laced with straw. Her red hand
high against the door has found
his forehead raging with the flu.

One autumn when the sky was maize
his uncle led him to the woods
and showed him how the pines
reveal the wind he could not feel.

His stand is perfect, but the deer to which
he is a death as random as a memory
has not appeared. He curls his toes,

tucks his hands inside his coat,
and rocks so slightly with a tender moan
that is swallowed by the distant whine
of tires on the road.

Advent Thoughts: Perry City Road

Something through the windbreak,
something like white leaves
lofted on a finger of the wind
settles to a lake of gulls
gleaning corn the cutter left.

These fields and trees descending
as if patterns on a quilt of snow.
Here and there, blue ropes of chimneys
climb to the blue air, and far below
mergansers glide into Cayuga's smoke
in such silence that the world
might hear its pulse.

Today these ordinary wonders
are the way to work, and yet
in advent nothing can be left alone
that might become a tabula
upon which hope has been explained.

That pearl above the black arms
of an elm might be the Morning Star.
And then, and then...
to say each calendar's a rivulet
that drips into the gorge
where even light has sought its level
and departed to the *Hand of God*,
where each eye opens
sown upon the only galaxy
it cannot see.

Advent from the Blue Water Bridge

Today I drive across the span of someone's hope,
the one that happened. Two million vehicles a year,
whose people all see something here.
Today a single freighter sorties north
into Huron's wide and frigid blue
toward a promise of the Soo...and then?

While south across the land's gray stew
where nothing is as once it was
the stack-plumes bend as white as bones
in the same wind that sings from rigging,
The year is nearly gone, and we shall see...
In a week, if the ship is safe for then,
resting in Duluth, its cargo traded,
its sailors murmuring in dreams
under quilts and wreaths and stars, can we say
that life has kept a bargain with a few?

Two million vehicles a year,
whose people all see something here,
and in each a moment waits
when we're stopped by what we see
and left to wonder, "Whose hope was this?"
Below, the shops are lit with expectation.

And yet we always wish for good beyond each end.
My father told me stories.
So somewhere, still, the Interurban cars
have chimed and slowed, their passengers
about to dance among the platform's snows.

What might they make of this construction?
It's so familiar, the way our souls
adsorb to steel and stone
and make our wishes over things we see.

I watch that solitary vessel counting miles
as the whitecaps build. From its deck
I'm lost into the eastern sky beneath a star.
It is a story that we tell.

In Advent

For Louis Adams 1919-1998

From the bridle trail, whitetail flash
among the trees and disappear. Or perhaps
the low sun glances off the scruffy barks.
Each version has its possibilities
as something fills the blank desire
to be a story we believe in
because we can recall a moment when
the deer were real, or the plays of sun
on one tree more particular.

Is it only human to imagine
that each story has its shadow
just as true? Nature gives us
only what we glean, a thing to hope for.

When the tide leaves, the sand emerges
with its worn or broken flotsam
lost or found by accident.
When the sun bleeds into the night's black silt
we wake the stars. We think,
"If not one thing, then another…"

A year ago, waiting for my father,
I watched a mother and her daughter
leave oncology, silent as willows,
their baggy woolen caps a powdered blue,
the petals of their awful skin
reflected in the doors as amber.
Their taxi vanished in the Cleveland rain.
I caught his eyes, and for the first time in my life
that I didn't know the answer

I asked him if he were afraid. *No.*

My arm still lifts him from the sheets to drink.
This trail winds near the stream
whose pools he ran to as a wild boy.
The color of his mother's plum trees in a dream.

Father, even hope is a construction
as you knew so perfectly.
Last night Orion walked above me,
a story that you showed me long ago.

Each day, each place, I set these memories
like cairns that mark your simple gift
of what to hope for, how to be. As if
we were the children of our own brief lives.

Faces on the Orange Line

Each face hangs like a flower dried to silence
in the sallow air of Back Bay Station.

As if by decree, we sway as the car sways.
The ads above our eyes are fixed as mirrors

of something we have learned too well.
A folded Herald covers some pink spill.

This could be a reliquary's dream of life,
each flower with a story no one tells.

But one round, almond daughter
jerks free of her mother's sleeve.

"Nooo, Mama! No!
I want to go now!"

The Music of Advent at North Station

Here you could wait for anything
and be surprised, even this strange music.
They call a train as he clacks and slides,
his face a black mollusk beneath his dreads.
He's humming something sweet as coal,
trailing a hood of no color on earth.
Glass doors whoosh open, lifting a yellow wrapper.
Two shoppers pass and scold each other.
Next to me a limo driver rocks back on his heels
and squawks into his phone,
"I've waited twenty minutes. She's not here."
Here you could wait for the music
of a single star in a slab of dirty marble.

Yesterday, as the train passed Exeter, New Hampshire,
the sky flew by, a milky tea in sepia.
The dizzying stutter of poplar and fir
flew by and opened to a glimpse of burial—
not a dozen mourners, clumped like blue shrubbery.
I was still thinking that those elusive
diamonds of the Merrimac were a thing alive.
So why wouldn't I see you again for the first
time, so like a flower yet unnamed.

True and Untrue at Christmas

On this morning, of all mornings, he could not
remember any lie he'd ever told.
But sitting at the table in his ex-wife's kitchen
and staring up the slope of the yard,
he can watch a red-tail warring with some crows
above the broken cans of Genny Lite
his son had stacked beneath a yew.
They had been targets for his grandson's
Christmas rifle and glitter now
like melted ornaments.

Alone at the table he stares absently,
his own hands somehow as red
as if he had been busy pawing snow.
From another room he hears a radio.
He knows that he's not welcome here.

Of course, once upon a time, there was
a brother who stole his food, his money,
then his sight, and then his soul. And so
he clasped his life from tree to tree,
or so the story goes. At last he found
the whiskey dripping from an oak,
like the sweet fire of the whole world.

He used to use the mornings for forgiveness.
Last night, among his family, he had crooned
his own old song of explanation
*That was my territory—all the way
from Binghamton to Hammondsport.*
It is the music that he knows by heart.

As for the rest, he would simply tell you
that his love was always too large
or too small for his family to bear.

If the light in his bourbon resembles
the light in his eyes, such an old story
is worth a quiet curse or two.

But it's Christmas morning, and a sliver
of sunlight plays upon the targets.
The birds have fled, and he is still here,
like something left behind a sigh.

The Feast of the Epiphany at North Chagrin

One hundred feet below this bridle path some teals and mallards gather in a pool hidden from almost anyone. My dog and I crouch together just to watch. It surprises me that she'd just watch, as if making up her mind about a brand new world, and so we crouch together barely breathing. The slate gray Cleveland dampness settles through the firs as if it were the ash of a prayer burned out. Like the blue and yellow clays, the endless singing waters of a world I knew when I was alone. Like home. But right now, dogs and ducks and I are safe from memories. What can we give you on this day of your birth? If you want to seem old, then seem old. If you must be dangerous and free, then let the world know you're leaving. If only this nearly perfect silence could decide something beyond itself. Below, a solitary mallard bobs over a little ice jam and into the stream beyond. Sometimes, watching is too much like waiting for the perfect now, too much like forgetting everything. A sigh in the distance too much like the swollen river to which we lit a candle and a wish. But here she's up and moving, sniffing the gravel for its history. For her, at least, the next moment is the next story.

Question for the Mind of Winter

How many sunsets
have bled an orange
so deep as this,
have caught you
dreaming your blue hands
into an embrace
remembered largely
for the shock
of cold starlight
feathered in
the corner
of a window
while she tells you
that for which
you've waited all
your life in a vision
that carries across
the blue snow that
lies upon a hill
that you remember
as clearly
as your name,
as gentle
and welcome
as death?

Kiska's Taste in Turds

It's a level of discrimination
that lies beyond my grasp.
Here at the Chittenango Service Area,
neither rain, nor snow, nor sleet,
nor all of that can stay this
Siberian from her appointed rounds.

As the sleet sneaks down my collar,
I ponder the mystery of her choices—
which turds she deems worth squatting on
and adding to the story, and which
she passes with a sniff almost of derision.

At least she's not some damned fecophile
like Bruno, an old housemate's
German Wire-Haired,
who never met a turd he wouldn't scarf:
dog, horse, bear, even turkey buzzard pudding!

Not my Kiska! She's into judgments
and narratives that I'll never understand.
And she looks back at me with one blue eye,
one gold, with her half smile, as if to say,
"You need to trust me on this. There are
some things you're not equipped to know."

The Light of Advent Falls across Sandusky County

There was a story here in Ohio.
From the distance of this road
the breaks of forest shrink like worlds,
remnant dreams of someone's darker love.

Some miles north
across the bleach of stubble fields
a white thumb of steam presses
down on something I can't see,
where sky is snow's gray prophecy.

You can stand there if you wish.
It's easy. It's November,
and the sky is open to lament,
for beneath it we have loved
what we could, named nearly everything
except that which we must forgive.

Perhaps we've told ourselves too much,
the stories drowned or dead of thirst,
or poisoned into perfect blooms…
who can remember? Or was it
the sweet, gold dreams of silos,
purchased with a wretchedness
too cold to bear, that broke
the egret's wing and left it there,
a dark branch, a prayer.

The mile markers pass like years;
That sky might loom as empty as a mirror

except that here, in your eyes, the white wings
unfold. Here, in your grey eyes,
the white wings unfold as stars.

So let us hold something for a while,
in silence, knowing only what it is.

A New Year in the Empire of Shadows

How much does a shadow weigh?
This black locust sighs against
the eaves in a midnight wind.
Far off, an owl mourns an hour
rendered darkly on the snow,
mourns a loss more essential,
how it learned its memories.

As I stood in the black cold
last night, I watched a shadow
like a wound beneath your eye.
Was it just the way you turned
as that darkness found your hands
at rest in some dishwater
where each story burst like foam?

Tonight you rise from the new
snow in my yard, beneath the
bright leaf of moon, as if you
would remember, would explain.
Even grief has a shadow.
For such stories we require
more than ordinary light.

The owl's talon clasps some fur.
Let me tell you something dear
to some shadow. A friend once
sang an old year to ashes
while ghost hounds shifted closer
to the fire no longer feared
before their eyes closed to dreams.

Song for the Winter Solstice at Chagrin

Tonight we bade the river listen to our wishes.
Tonight we lit two candles and some incense
in the snow beside the river's tongue.

So why should I remember now a lost
December when a ridge above the Cuyahoga
burned at dusk like purple grain?
Why recall the strangers' faces
salted there like passing moons?

For then I dreamed of tossing boughs across the ice
of an elsewhere solitary as a choice—
leaning to darkness or to light like planets
in a season come and gone so long ago
even the ancient webs of stars
have no stories that explain.
In that dream an angel or a puppy
might have spun the boughs for meaning.
But no, it was a dream of silences and waiting,
a faint moon's shadow like a sleeping boy.

In our years of dreams and wars the world
can seem too clear for light to help at all.
And yet tonight we knelt in snow
and watched those humble flames until our joys
sang like wolves above our sorrows
Once we've waited long enough,
hope is not so difficult to understand.
Later, I watched you across the table,
your eyes like grey flowers in a star.

Advent at the Port of Galilee

Not for the first time does he linger in his car
as the sun's last flare is extinguished in
the black Sound. Across the lot behind him
two diners gaze from George's window, where
lights are blinking on a little tree,
carols that make the waitress hard to hear.
A lone purse seiner churns through darkness
on the rising tide. The running lights
reveal the slicker of a man astern
who is bent a little, coiling something.
Across the way some windows light Jerusalem.
Perhaps he does not need God to make
something out of nothing after all.
A day ago, a year ago, perhaps today,
he drove above the frozen Mohawk Valley,
down there crows drifted to the snow
like parachutes. Once he told a lover
he was coming home across these mountains,
floating like a bubble in the wind.
He doesn't need the stars,
and tonight there are none.
To be this perfectly alone is so much
like the start of one thing or another
that it feels like a choice.
If he cracks his window, he can hear
the fading slap of the seiner's wake.
He remembers that he loved her face,
candled by the moon, as much when he saw it
as when he did not. It was there, waiting.
Perhaps hope is just his situation.
It could have been a seal, that water's kiss,
the black eyes cradling someone's light
as if it might just shatter.

Advent at the Hospice of the Western Reserve

What can we hold inside a room?
Some cards and pictures, two balloons,
a rosary coiled like a dragon,
and every memory she can bear.
Outside three gulls ride above
a swath of roses bloomed from warmth
we can't explain. It is December, after all.

Here is the shortest season, unfolding
in the space between heartbeats attenuated
in the space of a last, good dream.
Down the hall in the rotunda murals circle,
cast in clouds that shift as our familiars—a dog,
a door, a reverie of being held,
an angel studying a page.
My father died here, too.
In another life he told me,
"Hope is what we make from nothing."
I have nothing left to ask her.
She holds a picture of their wedding.
She is a color I can't recognize.

A voice is singing from a carol
"…in the bleak midwinter…"
And now she forgives even tenderness.

An Argument of Hope along a Passage to the Allegheny

Hope will be gentle. Hope will be wise.
Hope will spread wider than all the earth's skies.
Words knit on a stocking and pinned to a tree.
In Seneca Falls the wet snow gathers like a paste
on the lock of the old canal, its water as quiet as coal.
So is hope a destination or a memory?
Seen through a salt-streaked windshield, a landfill
as a mountain, yard signs staggered south in red
and blue: *No Sovereign Nation, No Reservation.*

There is no resolution in leaving Romulus behind.
The vacant Depot shades the white deer in its scrub,
their red eyes pulsing through the thorns.
Here, above the Hand of God, each mile brings a story no
one wished to happen quite the way it does.
Three hunters flecked with orange haunt a tree line,
pausing in a crude isosceles to hear a rasp
of crows in an oak's black branches, a whine
of tires from a pickup rocking in the mud.

In Ovid three men in Carhartts stand on a fire truck,
hang wreaths and lights above the empty stores. One
steps down to judge an angle a bit more carefully,
behind him a window of Properties for Sale.
From Hector to Lodi, from Lodi to the Glen,
past the rows of sleeping vines, past Lamoka,
past Keuka, west along the Southern Tier,
the ribbons of the Allegheny merge into a river
that leads anywhere. Who can tell such stories
       and believe?

Take one breath, and then another.
Here is the crease of sunlight burning
between the mountains and the clouds.
Here is the sound of water
    spilling to the world.

Indications of Advent on LaDue Reservoir

My kayak glides into December
like a bright red blade in a landscape
faded grey and brown and green beneath
a sky that hovers like a single cloud
as edged and delicate as mica.

Yesterday I watched my mother slap
her palm against her heart and fix her eyes
hard into her mother's century—
shawls billowing chenille and silk,
a row of glads like acolytes
leaning from a breeze that cannot end.

How strangely might the World insist…
There was a chord with someone's name.
There was a vase that spilled its prayers;
they rolled like candles. They were stars.

A string of gleaming decoys spin and bob
unnaturally in the freshening wind.
All brands of hope float here in ways
so small you'd think that living any life
at all was just a matter of addition.
But the mergansers are not fooled
and cluster near the dam far out of range.
I can hear the whispered curses in the reeds,
and I remember that the reedy hours that wave
and ring us all our lives hold every
whisper ever heard or lost or dreamed….

In the middle of this water I just stop

and feel the drift to stillness nearly perfect
but for me, balanced on an edge so fragile
between acceptance and tomorrow
as the wind and waves ripple into agitation.
It can be too late for wonder.
Still, to feel blessed just now…who knows?

The paddle dips and pulls,
a breath of water tracing the parabola
towards the longer lights of winter,
towards home, wherever that is.

An Advent Dream Begins in Majuro

This sheeting squall has draped a shroud
upon such lights that were as watch fires moored
across the black lagoon, a perfect darkness.
Last night, waiting for a ride I caught instead as glimpse
a pickup streaming, hung with boughs of ironwood,
a plastic reindeer wrapped with strings of lights
and strapped atop the cab. The driver, in profile,
showed a grin that still escapes description,
and I remember how it is to be a stranger anywhere.

Once it was walking the frozen stubble
marking last year's corn, beside the black ice
of a drainage ditch, watched by crimson eyes
atop a distant silo. Once it was a red clay right of way while
the CHESSIE rumbled northward as its own terrifying wind.
And now, as the squall has fled,
some wondrous silence as the world is reconstructed
from abyss — coral heads like patens in the moonlight,
the ships and fires, the dark straw of the islets.

I've heard it said that there is no dream of now, but still I
wonder. Wake and sweep a hand across the longitudes, and
walk with the ghosts my mother sees,
lying in her frailty where now is one more breath.

Once it was to lean against an elm and watch the hunter
climb its winter limbs, a story just impossible.
What a thing it is, even happiness, this waiting!
Remember how it is to be a stranger anywhere,
or a man with a reindeer on his cab.

The Effect of Snow on Dreams

I felt it coming long before I woke,
snow sifting through the blue darkness,

netting a streetlamp as a silver bird,
falling, falling into my dream.

There its slow accumulation
alters nothing.

We are wound in one another;
In your eyes the weather

we have awaited for so long
      approaches.

Advent Graves at All Souls Cemetery

It seems that I am walking on a frozen steppe
and not this rolling country east of home.
The distant cedars breathe and spin the snow
as filigrees. The stone evangelists each gaze
upon a corner of this plat I know by heart.

For a little while the rules are slackened to allow
the varnished crosses, the wreaths with crimson ribbons,
the linen orchids and chrysanthemums.
One grave even has a small, blue chimney
with a stocking and a photograph—a boy in khaki.
It feels like a riot of remembrance without words.

I wouldn't lie about such things, not in
this sacred ground in which the syllables
of Eastern Europe sleep in their last America.

They need two wolves to howl and prance
a Czárdás and remember—the wedding
dances on linoleum, the lamps and sparks
and whirring lathes consigned unto
the last shifts of their lives, in which
the yellow buses growl past TAPCO,
Eaton Axle, Fisher Body, Chase Brass—
all grown filmy as the cloud of toil and beads
from cuts that drip into the lubricating oil.
The morning songs of beer and cabbage and anger.

It was that cloud they shared he couldn't bear
and couldn't breathe. For years I watched him
wander to each labor as if searching for his tribe.

The wind stings my neck and scrapes across the graves.
Can I stand here as the better life he dreamed?
I know that forty years ago we left a job
as numb as ice and watched the winter sun
plunge beneath the Cuyahoga's purple ridge
to leave behind a single star I still hold near.
Waiting there or here, it is my only answer.

Advent Dreams in the Garden of Snows

If you had watched him leave his door,
as the moon shone through him,
you might have thought he was a ghost
who had no destination. Impossible, of course,
And yet, you'd see the arms limp at his sides,
his eyes so plainly cast towards memory.
His neighbors' happy lights blink to him of losses
so intense that anywhere surpasses now....

Yesterday his car slowed at a crossroads,
no one else in sight, the only motion
the hop and peck of crows amidst a stubble bleached
as brown as tea, clouds hung low in freezing fog.
And he whispered as if someone were near.
"Is such a place as this the field of hope"?

At morning he had left a diner, gliding
past a table full of ladies almost chanting
to a centerpiece of holly, the rhythms
of their voices harmless and incessant,
a carol of birds written without rests.

Why, then, should he remember that owl on fire,
a hunger swept across the headlights' beams,
hunting, trailing grains of silver in its wash,
white sides of the pines bowed as messengers?
They might have caught him counting flakes
into a different dream, two boys bundled
in the Mercury, naming constellations

until the words return: *Even hope is a construction.*
As is also its desire, longing for just one star.
So he wakes upon a globe of ice,
walking in a garden where the snow defines
the furrows as frozen swells and braids
    the arborvitae.

Sixty feet away, beside a broken trellis, his dog
paws at the crust, grinning with mock ferocity.
It is a thing to which he must attend.

Advent in a Wind of Memory

That Sunday in November framed him
jogging in a field on which his father played
more than fifty years before. He could
almost see him, standing on a sideline
while the scrubs got in their work,
right shoulder stooped, a crooked smile
that could mask anything, elusive
as a ghost of its own imagining.

As the laps grew shorter he could feel
the wind's chill worming through his ears,
a paddler's sign it's time to turn around.
He stopped, then crouched above the soggy turf,
gazing past new buildings bricked a cankered orange
to the line of oaks beyond, their stubborn leaves
lifting and dipping like grackles.
Leaves as birds; birds as lovers…

In what seems more than a life ago,
in a record store on Prospect Avenue,
he watched transfixed as a black kid
swung a girl so sweetly to his lips
and held her in the very breath of life;
while he himself was still too young
to know what he could love, not love.

Yet, still, he was always stoked with dreams.
Even years later, exhausted, digging clays
in the bottom of a trench, he thought
that he could find the wormhole to his real world.
The woman at the bank had told him,
"Sorry, I could never date a laborer."

So what is like a candle that never
   burns away?
In moments then and since he understands
that he's been searching losses for their treasures.
To have loved what perishes should make him
sadder than it does, despite his careful sighs.
The leaves...the birds...the lovers.

He is startled from this vision by a curse
and sees a man as about old as he
with puffs of breath, holding broken strings,
chasing a brown diamond of a kite that
pinwheels madly to the parking lot. Finally,
the man has halted, hands upon his knees.
He is smiling. Even the curls as gray as ash
trailing from his cap do seem to smile
in this light. The kite is gone.
   And he is smiling.

CPSIA information can be obtained
at www.ICGtesting.com
Printed in the USA
FFOW02n1827291216
30739FF